P9-BIW-537

FANTASTIC PHENOMENA

Children's Press®
An Imprint of Scholastic Inc.
New York   Toronto London   Auckland Sydney
Mexico City   New Delhi   Hong Kong
Danbury, Connecticut

Book production: Educational Reference Publishing

Book design: Nancy Hamlen D'Ambrosio

Science adviser: Jennifer A. Roth, M.A.

Library of Congress Cataloging-in-Publication Data

Fantastic Phenomena.
     p. cm. — (Experiment with science)
  Includes bibliographical references and index.
ISBN-13: 978-0-531-18543-8 (lib. bdg.)   978-0-531-18759-3 (pbk.)
ISBN-10: 0-531-18543-5 (lib. bdg.)   0-531-18759-4 (pbk.)
  1. Science—Experiments—Juvenile literature. 2.
Physics—Experiments—Juvenile literature. I. Children's Press (New
York, N.Y.) II. Title.
  Q164.F26 2008
  507.8—dc22
                                    2007020447

1 2 3 4 5 6 7 8 9 10 R 17 16 15 14 13 12 11 10 09 08

CONTENTS

Bubble Shapes

Learn the science behind monster-sized bubbles!

Hungry Microbes

Watch what happens when a decaying banana releases gas!

Tornado in a Bottle

Be amazed at the fantastic tornado you can make.

Creating Craters!

Find out what happens when a meteorite hits the surface of the Moon.

States of Water

See how solids, liquids, and gases behave.

Lots of Lava!

How does lava form? Stand back . . . and find out!

Vacuum Power!

Grab a helper and demonstrate how water flows up into treetops.

Static Electricity Lightning

You'll be "shocked" to see how you can create a miniature lighting bolt.

Total Eclipse!

Demonstrate what happens in an actual eclipse, and learn how to view one *safely*.

FANTASTIC PHENOMENA

Why does a volcano erupt? What causes lightning? Where do meteorites and craters come from? What causes matter to decompose? Volcanoes, lightning, meteorites and craters, and decomposed matter are all things that we have seen or at least read about. But to scientists, they are phenomena—exceptional events that interest them and, most of the time, can be explained by them. To many of us, these phenomena are fantastic as well—we can see them and they're amazing, but how they happen is usually beyond our understanding.

 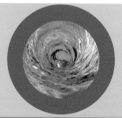   

Each experiment in this book leads you through the steps you must take to reach a successful conclusion based on scientific results. There are also important symbols you should recognize before you begin your experiment. Here's how the experiments are organized:

Name of experiment

Goal, or purpose, of the experiment

A **You Will Need** box provides a list of supplies you'll need to complete the experiment, as well as the approximate amount of time the experiment should take.

Here's What You Will Do gives step-by-step

instructions for working through the experiment.

Here's What's Happening explains the science behind the experiment—and what the conclusion should be.

Mess Factor shows you on a scale of 0 to 5 just how messy the experiment might be (a good thing to know before you begin!).

Science Safety: Whenever you see this caution symbol, read the instructions and be extra careful.

That's about to change! What really makes the phenomena in this book fantastic is that all of them can be duplicated in the laboratory.

We should consider ourselves lucky that we haven't actually seen some of these phenomena close up. Who would want to be standing on the rim of a volcano when it erupts, or near a tornado as it roars toward you, or in the path of an incoming meteorite? Other phenomena, such as a total eclipse of the Sun, are awesome events that happen only once in a great while. Some of the most interesting phenomena are the ones that we take for granted. Why does water turn to ice? How does water get to the top leaves of a tree? What makes a bubble so special?

In this book, we'll get the lowdown on all these fantastic phenomena—and we'll do it by making them happen right in front of us. We'll see how each phenomenon works and why. And we'll do it all in the lab. Get ready for some fantastic fun!

This symbol means that you should ask an adult to help you or be nearby as you conduct the experiment. Although all the experiments in this book are appropriate and safe for kids to do, whenever you're handling anything that might be sharp or hot, it's important to have adult supervision.

ADULT

In the back of the book, **Find Out More** offers suggestions of other books to read on the subject of fantastic phenomena, and cool Web sites to check out. The **Glossary** (pages 30-31) provides definitions of the highlighted words appearing throughout this book. Finally, the **Index** is the place to go to find exactly what you're looking for.

Here are some important tips before you begin your experiment:

- Check with an adult.
- Read the experiment all the way through.
- Gather everything you need.
- Choose and prepare your "lab" work area.
- Wash and dry your hands.
- Use only clean containers for your experiments.
- Keep careful notes of everything you do and see.
- Stop and ask an adult if you aren't sure what to do.
- When you're finished, clean up your work area completely, and wash your hands!

BUBBLE SHAPES

HAVE YOU EVER NOTICED THAT FLOATING BUBBLES ARE ALWAYS ROUND? IN THIS EXPERIMENT, YOU'LL FIND OUT WHY—AND ALSO LEARN WHAT MAKES BUBBLES SO SCIENTIFICALLY SPECIAL.

YOU WILL NEED

- ❑ measuring cup
- ❑ 1 cup liquid dish soap
- ❑ 6 cups lukewarm water
- ❑ large baking dish
- ❑ spoon
- ❑ wire hanger

TIME: 30 MINUTES

MESS FACTOR: 2

HERE'S WHAT YOU WILL DO

1 Pour 1 cup of dish soap and 6 cups of water into your baking pan. Slowly stir until the ingredients look evenly blended. (Try not to make bubbles just yet!)

2 Bend the hook of the hanger into a handle that you can put your finger through. Stretch and shape the body of the hanger into a square or a triangle—*not a circle*. This is your bubble wand.

3 Dip your giant wand into the soap mixture. Take it out, swoosh the wand through the air, and start making bubbles!

4 Notice the shape that the bubbles take when they start to leave the wand. Then look at the shape they take the instant they break free.

HERE'S WHAT'S HAPPENING

Surface tension is the scientific explanation for why the soapy water clings to the edges of your bubble wand. Surface tension is a pulling force that makes water molecules hold themselves together. Your bubble begins to form in the shape of the wand. (Bubbles need air inside to keep them from collapsing right away.) But once the bubble breaks free from the wand, surface tension pulls the soapy water together, and the bubble forms the least stretchy shape it can. That shape is a ball, or sphere.

TORNADO IN A BOTTLE

WHAT DO A TORNADO AND A WHIRLPOOL HAVE IN COMMON? EACH IS AN EXAMPLE OF A VORTEX. IN THIS EXPERIMENT, YOU'LL CREATE A WHIRLPOOL TORNADO IN A BOTTLE.

Tornadoes are violent windstorms that can be various sizes, shapes, and colors. Most tornadoes occur in the United States, mainly in the Midwest.

YOU WILL NEED

- ❑ 2 soda bottles (2-liter size)
- ❑ 3-4 cups water
- ❑ food coloring (optional)
- ❑ large pinch of pepper
- ❑ 6-inch-wide duct tape

TIME: 30 MINUTES

MESS FACTOR: 1

HERE'S WHAT YOU WILL DO

1 Fill one of the bottles three-quarters full of water. (You can add a few drops of food coloring for fun.) Add a large pinch of pepper. Swirl to mix.

2 Place the second bottle, mouth to mouth (the part you drink from), on top of the first. Make sure the openings match up exactly. Tape the mouths together firmly with the duct tape.

3 Turn over the joined bottles and give them a quick swirl to start the water spinning. You should see a vortex (a powerful, spinning current of water) start to form in the top bottle.

4 Repeat. This time, try to keep your eyes on the flakes of pepper. Are they moving faster at the wide top of the whirling vortex or at its narrow bottom?

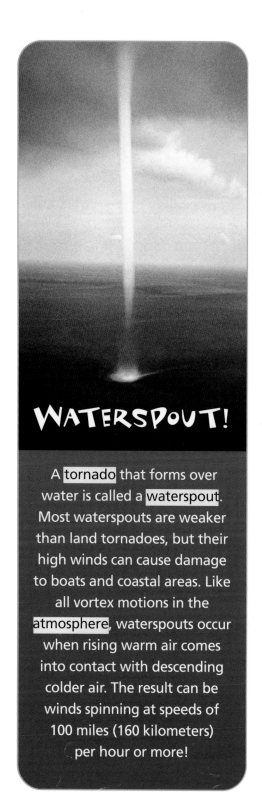

WATERSPOUT!

A tornado that forms over water is called a waterspout. Most waterspouts are weaker than land tornadoes, but their high winds can cause damage to boats and coastal areas. Like all vortex motions in the atmosphere, waterspouts occur when rising warm air comes into contact with descending colder air. The result can be winds spinning at speeds of 100 miles (160 kilometers) per hour or more!

IT'S A WHIRLPOOL!

Whirlpools can happen when water currents collide. Ocean tides sometimes trigger whirlpools when the incoming tide hits the outgoing tide at an angle (not directly head-on). In the same way, you get a miniature whirlpool in a sink or bathtub when the water rushes down an open drain.

HERE'S WHAT'S HAPPENING

The vortex that you created in the bottle demonstrates the forces that shape a tornado. As you noticed in your bottled tornado, the narrow bottom of the spinning vortex spins faster than its wider top. This is just what happens with a real tornado. As a tornado begins to take shape, the narrow part of the funnel spins faster than the wider part of the funnel. This funnel shape is what helps push a tornado to the ground.

STATES OF WATER

WATER IS THE ONLY SUBSTANCE ON EARTH THAT'S FOUND IN ALL POSSIBLE FORMS—GAS, LIQUID, AND SOLID—UNDER NATURAL CONDITIONS. BEGINNING WITH A CUP OF ICE, YOU'LL LEARN ABOUT THE THREE STATES OF MATTER.

YOU WILL NEED

- measuring cup
- 1 cup ice
- quart-size zipper-lock bag
- rolling pin
- ceramic mug
- 1/4–1/2 cup salt
- spoon

TIME:
1 DAY

MESS FACTOR:

1

Heat from the warming rays of the Sun turn these icicles—water in its frozen, or solid form—to plain liquid water.

HERE'S WHAT YOU WILL DO

1 Measure about a cup of ice and put it in the plastic bag. Squeeze out as much air as you can, and zip closed. Lay the bag on a counter or on the floor, and crush the ice with a rolling pin.

2 Fill the mug two-thirds with crushed ice. Add salt until it reaches about an inch below the rim. Stir well. Let the mug sit undisturbed for 15 minutes to a half hour.

3 You should see a frosty-looking solid forming on the outside of the mug. Scrape some into a spoon. You end up with a liquid, right? Put the spoon with the liquid in a spot where it won't be disturbed, and leave it for 24 hours. Is the liquid still there when you check back?

THE WATER CYCLE

Water rises from the oceans as vapor, collects in clouds, falls as rain, seeps into and runs over the ground, and finally returns to the oceans, where the cycle begins again. This cycling of the Earth's water is important because there is never any new water. The quantity of water has not changed since before the time of the dinosaurs.

HoW CAN iCE BE DRY?

In changing from solid to **gas**, most substances pass through a liquid state. Sometimes, however, a substance goes directly from solid to gas—a process known as **sublimation**. Dry ice, which is solid **carbon dioxide**, is the best-known example of this phenomenon; it sublimes—changes from a solid to a gas—at −109.3° F (−78.5° C). It is called dry ice because it can be used to keep objects cold without getting them wet!

HERE'S WHAT'S HAPPENING

All **matter** in the world exists in just three forms—solid, liquid, or gas. Solids have a definite shape. Liquids flow and take the shape of their containers. Gases spread out in all directions. In this experiment, you see that a change in **temperature** can change water from one state to another. The temperature of ice drops below freezing when salt is added. This causes **water vapor** (a gas) to **condense** (turn into liquid water) out of the air and freeze into ice (a solid) on the outside of the mug. When you scraped the ice into the spoon, it warmed up and melted into liquid water. When you left the water in the open air for a day, it **evaporated** back into a gas.

VACUUM POWER!

IN THIS EXPERIMENT, YOU'LL USE SUCTION TO FIND OUT HOW WATER FLOWS UP INTO THE TREETOPS.

YOU WILL NEED

- ❏ 2-quart pitcher
- ❏ 2 quarts grape juice
- ❏ 2 feet of clean, flexible tubing
- ❏ 3 drinking glasses
- ❏ a helper

TIME: 30 MINUTES

MESS FACTOR: 2

How does water get up to the leaves at the top of the largest tree in the world? Water evaporates out of the leaves, and this creates a vacuum that draws up more water through the tree's trunk.

HERE'S WHAT YOU WILL DO

Arrange three glasses on a table. Fill the pitcher half full of juice. Put one end of the tubing into the juice.

Suck on the other end of the tube to draw juice into the tube. Stop just before the juice reaches your lips. Quickly cap the open end with your thumb. Have your helper lift the pitcher so its bottom is higher than the glasses. Make sure the tube stays in the juice.

Hold the capped end of the tube over the first glass. Remove your thumb and fill the glasses! Be sure to recap the open end of the tube as you move from glass to glass.

HERE'S WHAT'S HAPPENING

Sucking on the tube created a vacuum that drew the juice up the tube against gravity. Once the juice passed over the tube's highest point (the rim of the pitcher), gravity pulled the liquid down into the glasses.

In a living plant, water evaporates out of the leaves and creates a vacuum that draws more water up through hollow tubes in the plant's stem, called xylems. The suction, or drawing power, will continue as long as juice keeps pouring out of the tube (or as long as water keeps evaporating out of a plant's leaves).

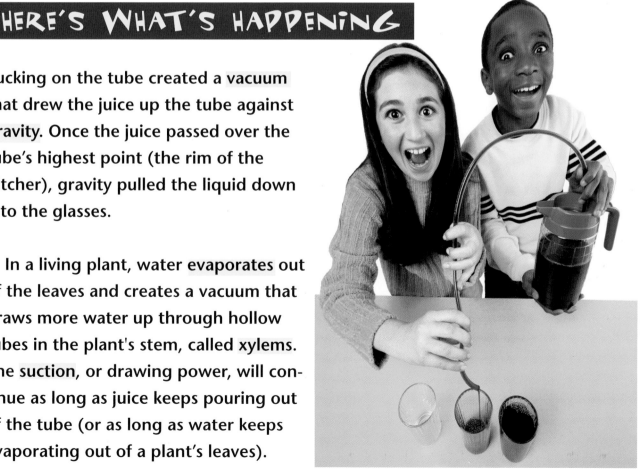

TOTAL ECLIPSE!

IN A SOLAR ECLIPSE, THE MOON PASSES DIRECTLY BETWEEN THE SUN AND EARTH. IN THIS EXPERIMENT, YOU'LL DEMONSTRATE WHAT HAPPENS IN AN ACTUAL ECLIPSE.

A total solar eclipse occurs when the Moon passes in front of the Sun and completely blocks it. Only the Sun's corona (the halo of light) is visible.

YOU WILL NEED

- ❑ 1 stick modeling clay
- ❑ pencil
- ❑ baseball
- ❑ a helper
- ❑ small flashlight
- ❑ darkened room

TIME:
20 MINUTES

MESS FACTOR:
0

HERE'S WHAT YOU WILL DO

1 Roll some clay into a ball about the size of a cherry. Stick it onto the eraser end of a pencil. This represents the Moon.

2 Hold the "Moon" in front of the baseball. The ball represents Earth. Give your helper the flashlight for the Sun. (Take a look at the photo on the next page to see how everything should be lined up.)

3 Turn off the lights. Have your helper shine the flashlight toward the "Moon" from a couple of feet away. You should see a shadow on the ball.

Safely ▲ Observe an Eclipse!

Never look directly at the Sun, even during a partial eclipse! Direct sunlight can cause permanent eye damage, even blindness, in seconds. Not even sunglasses or camera filters will protect your eyes.

One safe way to view a solar eclipse is with a Sun viewer or pinhole projector. To make the Sun viewer, take two index cards or pieces of white cardboard. Puncture a small hole in one card. With your back to the Sun, hold this card so that sunlight passes through the hole and falls onto the second card. You'll see the eclipse projected in miniature on the paper!

After you have viewed the eclipse with your pinhole viewer, you will be able to see it again—safely and in detail—on television.

THE MOON ECLIPSES TOO!

In an eclipse of the Moon, or lunar eclipse, the Moon passes through the shadow that Earth casts out into space. During a lunar eclipse, Earth is positioned between the Sun and the Moon. As the Moon enters Earth's shadow, it grows dark because it is no longer lighted by the Sun. A lunar eclipse only occurs during a full moon.

HERE'S WHAT'S HAPPENING

A total solar eclipse occurs only when the Moon moves between the Sun and Earth, casting a shadow that moves across Earth from west to east. (This is the direction that the Moon moves in its orbit.) To observers in the shadow's path, the Moon briefly seems to cover the Sun's disk. Observers see only the Sun's bright corona. During a partial solar eclipse, observers see the Moon's curved shadow fall across one part of the Sun. An actual solar eclipse is visible for only a few minutes and only from a small portion of Earth.

HUNGRY MICROBES

DO YOU RECYCLE CANS, BOTTLES, AND PAPERS? WELL, NATURE RECYCLES, TOO! IN THIS EXPERIMENT, YOU'LL MEET THE BUSY WORKERS OF NATURE'S CLEAN-UP PROGRAM.

Mold has an important job! It recycles nutrients from decomposing food so that they are available to other organisms.

YOU WILL NEED

- ☐ 1 overripe banana
- ☐ small, narrow-mouth bottle
- ☐ balloon
- ☐ small rubber band

TIME: 1 WEEK

MESS FACTOR: 2

HERE'S WHAT YOU WILL DO

1 Peel the banana and squish it into the bottle (a one-serving drink bottle works well). Be sure to wash your hands and wipe off the bottle after you're done.

2 Stretch the opening of the balloon over the mouth of the bottle. Use the rubber band to make sure you have an airtight seal.

3 Put the bottle in a warm, sunny spot, such as an out-of-the-way windowsill. Check back every day for a week. The banana mash in the bottle should be shrinking. And the balloon should be expanding!

HERE'S WHAT'S HAPPENING

Have you ever wondered what happens to the fallen leaves, decayed plants, and other dead things that drop to the ground? Nature has its own way of taking care of them.

Tiny microbes called bacteria and mold spores fill the air around us. Some of these microbes can make us sick. But many play an important role. They help breakdown, or decompose, dead things. After eating and digesting their food (in this case, the banana), invisible microbes and mold in the bottle produce waste gases (mainly carbon dioxide and hydrogen). In this experiment, the microbes ate and digested the banana, causing it to decompose. The gases released by the microbes filled the bottle, causing the balloon to inflate.

CREATING CRATERS!

WHEN YOU LOOK AT A PHOTOGRAPH OF THE MOON, YOU CAN SEE CRATERS PRODUCED MILLIONS TO BILLIONS OF YEARS AGO. IN THIS ACTIVITY, YOU'LL DEMONSTRATE WHAT CAUSES CRATERS TO APPEAR.

The surface of the Moon is covered with craters. Almost all the craters on the Moon were formed by the impact of meteorites from space.

YOU WILL NEED

- ❏ pencil
- ❏ piece of paper
- ❏ large box
- ❏ 2–3 5-pound bags of flour
- ❏ newspaper
- ❏ different sized round objects (such as a marble, a baseball, a golf ball)
- ❏ ruler

TIME: 1 HOUR

MESS FACTOR: 2

HERE'S WHAT YOU WILL DO

1 Draw a table like the one shown on the next page.

2 Fill the box with 2 to 3 inches (5 to 8 centimeters) of flour. Gently shake the box to distribute the flour evenly over the bottom of the box, and smooth the surface of the flour. Place the box on a kitchen table or the floor. (Cover your work surface with newspaper.)

3 Measure your round objects. Record their diameters on the table.

4 Hold each object at shoulder height, and drop it (don't throw it!) into the box. Using your ruler, measure and record the diameter and depth of the flour "crater" made by the object.

5 Smooth the flour and repeat the activity. But this time, drop the objects from as far as you can reach above your head.

CRASH LANDING!

Small meteors often enter Earth's atmosphere. But almost all burn up in the air before they reach the ground (we call them shooting stars). One of the last big meteorites to hit Earth arrived some 50,000 years ago. It fell in the Arizona desert and left a ¾-mile- (1.2-kilometer-) wide crater, called the Barringer Meteorite Crater.

HERE'S WHAT'S HAPPENING

The Moon has a powdery surface somewhat like flour. Each crater on the Moon is a place where a meteorite hit the surface. In this experiment, you observed that larger meteorites create larger craters, just like on the Moon. A meteorite's speed of impact also affects the size of the crater it produces. Objects gain speed as they fall. So "meteors" dropped from above your head are moving faster when they hit the flour surface than are those dropped from shoulder height. The craters they produce are also larger.

Measurements

	Object Diam.	Crater Diam.	Crater Depth
marble			
baseball			
golf ball			

LOTS OF LAVA!

IN THIS ACTIVITY, YOU'LL BUILD A MINIATURE VOLCANO THAT DEMONSTRATES ALL THE EXCITEMENT OF A REAL VOLCANO, WITHOUT THE DANGER!

Red hot molten lava flows from the cone of Kilauea Volcano in Hawaii. Kilauea is the most active volcano in the world.

YOU WILL NEED

- ❏ funnel
- ❏ small bottle
- ❏ 1/2 cup baking soda
- ❏ 1 cup water
- ❏ red food coloring
- ❏ squirt of liquid dish soap
- ❏ large aluminum pan
- ❏ 5–10 pounds of sand
- ❏ 1 cup white vinegar

TIME: 45 MINUTES

MESS FACTOR: 4

HERE'S WHAT YOU WILL DO

1 Use the funnel to fill the bottle a quarter full with baking soda. Fill the bottle halfway with water. Add 10 drops of food coloring and a big squirt of liquid dish soap.

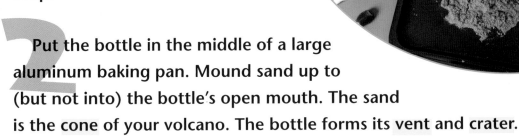

2 Put the bottle in the middle of a large aluminum baking pan. Mound sand up to (but not into) the bottle's open mouth. The sand is the cone of your volcano. The bottle forms its vent and crater.

3 Slowly pour vinegar into the buried bottle. When the vinegar combines with the baking soda, it will cause your volcano to erupt, and "lava" will begin to flow. Go easy! When the lava stops, you can add some more vinegar.

VISIT A REAL VOLCANO

There are about 500 active volcanoes around the world, not counting those beneath the sea. In the United States there are 170. Mount St. Helens in Washington State last erupted in 2004. Hawaii is home to five volcanoes. They are Kilauea (photo at left), Loihi, Mauna Loa, Hualalai, and Haleakala.

HERE'S WHAT'S HAPPENING

A real volcano erupts when hot gases and red-hot, molten rock, called lava, shoot up through a crack in Earth's crust. As this liquid rock flows, it burns everything it touches. Volcanoes occur along the boundaries of Earth's plates, where melted rock is forced upward from reservoirs of magma deep in the surface. In this experiment, your baking-soda volcano produces two of the gases seen in natural volcanoes: water vapor and carbon dioxide. When mixed together, the baking soda and vinegar produced carbon dioxide. As the gas expanded, it shot out of the bottle like an active volcano!

LAVA LAND
When Kilauea's lava enters the ocean, it cools and hardens to form new coastal land.

STATIC ELECTRICITY LIGHTNING

STATIC ELECTRICITY IS THE POWERHOUSE BEHIND ALL LIGHTNING STORMS. IN THIS EXPERIMENT, YOU'LL CREATE MINIATURE LIGHTNING BOLTS.

Lightning bolts can reach a temperature of 50,000° F (28,000° C). That's hotter than the surface of the Sun!

YOU WILL NEED

- ❑ transparent tape
- ❑ Styrofoam cup
- ❑ metal pie pan
- ❑ Styrofoam dinner plates
- ❑ wool sock
- ❑ dark room
- ❑ metal key

TIME: 30 MINUTES

MESS FACTOR: 1

HERE'S WHAT YOU WILL DO

1 Tape the cup securely to the inside of the pie pan—right in the center. Put a stack of several Styrofoam dinner plates upside down on a flat surface. Rub a wool sock across the back of the top plate for about 60 seconds. (Rub quickly and count very slowly.)

2 Pick up the pie pan by using the cup as a handle. Place the pie pan on top of the "charged" foam plates.

3 Turn off the light. Bring the key very close to the edge of the metal pan. Do you see a little spark of "lightning"?

HERE'S WHAT'S HAPPENING

Have you ever walked across a carpet in your stocking feet, and then touched something and gotten a shock? The same principle is happening here. Rubbing the sock over the plate transferred **static electricity** to the surface of the plate. The electricity moved through the pan and jumped to the key because metals **conduct**, or draw, electricity well. The **lightning** bolt that we usually see jumps from an electrically charged storm cloud to the ground (which contains metals).

FiND OUT MoRE

For more information on the science of fantastic phenomena, check out these books and Web sites:

BooKS

Allaby, Michael. *Tornadoes.* Dangerous Weather Series (2nd ed.). Facts on File, 2004.

Aronson, Billy. *Eclipses: Nature's Blackouts.* Watts, 1997.

Berger, Melvin, and Gilda Berger. *Why Do Volcanoes Blow Their Tops?: Questions and Answers about Volcanoes and Earthquakes.* Scholastic, 2000.

Branley, Franklyn M. *Flash, Crash, Rumble, and Roll.* HarperCollins, 1999.

Harper, Kristine. *The Mount St. Helens Volcanic Eruption.* Environmental Disasters Series. Facts on File, 2005.

Pascoe, Elaine. *Slime, Molds, and Fungi.* Nature Close-up Series. Thomson Gale, 1998.

Simon, Seymour. *The Moon* (rev. ed.). Simon & Schuster, 2003.

Spangenburg, Ray, and Kit Moser. *Meteors, Meteorites and Meteoroids: Out of This World.* Scholastic, 2002.

Tocci, Salvatore. *Experiments with the Sun and the Moon.* Scholastic, 2003.

WEB SiTES

DragonflyTV . PBS Kids Go!
pbskids.org/dragonflytv/show/mooncraters.html
How do Moon craters form? Find out on this page from Dragonfly TV, a PBS Kids Web site.

FEMA for Kids: Thunderstorms
www.fema.gov/kids/thunder.htm
Thunder won't hurt you, but lightning will, so have respect for thunderstorms! Learn more about thunderstorms, read up on lightning safety, and find out what to do if someone is struck by lightning.

FEMA for Kids: Volcanoes
www.fema.gov/kids/volcano.htm
Find out all about volcanoes at this special site for kids.

Inside Tornadoes Multimedia @ *National Geographic Magazine*
www7.nationalgeographic.com/ngm/0506/feature6/multimedia.html
See the first ever video from inside a tornado. From National Geographic.

NOVA Online/Hawaii - Born of Fire
www.pbs.org/wgbh/nova/hawaii/
Find out what it's like to be right next to an active volcano and learn about lava, lava sampling, and dating lava. A PBS Nova site.

StarChild: A Learning Center for Young Astronomers
starchild.gsfc.nasa.gov
Learn the basics of the solar system and the universe. From NASA. Includes many images and activities at elementary and middle grade levels.

WonderNet—Solutions
chemistry.org/portal/Chemistry?PID=wondernet display.html&DOC=wondernet\activities\ solutions\solutions.html
You've probably dissolved some type of solid, such as sugar or salt, in water. Did you know that liquids and gases can also dissolve? Try some activities to learn more about dissolving and why it is important. From the American Chemical Society.

GLOSSARY

A

atmosphere the mixture of gases that surrounds a planet.

B

bacteria simple, one-celled organisms; the oldest and most common form of life on Earth.

C

carbon dioxide a colorless and odorless gas that is a mixture of carbon and oxygen.

condense to change from a gas into a liquid.

conduct to allow electricity, heat, or sound to pass through.

cone (volcanic) a sloping mountain formed by ash and lava.

corona a ring of light seen around a shining object, such as the Sun.

crater (volcanic) the bowl-shaped opening of a volcano.

currents flows of air or water in motion.

D

decompose to rot or decay.

diameters straight lines through the centers of a circle, from one side to another.

E

evaporated, evaporates changed from a liquid into a gas.

G

gases substances, such as air, that will spread to fill any space that contains them.

gravity the force that pulls things down toward the surface of the Earth and keeps them from floating away into space.

H

hydrogen a colorless gas that is lighter than air and catches fire easily.

L

lightning a flash of light in the sky that appears when electricity moves between clouds or between a cloud and the ground.

liquid one of three states of matter; liquids flow and take the shape of their containers.

lunar eclipse occurs when Earth comes between the Sun and the Moon so that all or part of the Moon's light is blocked out.

M

magma melted rock found beneath Earth's surface.

matter anything that has weight and takes up space, such as a solid, a liquid, or a gas.

meteorites parts of a meteor that strike the surface of a moon or planet.

meteors pieces of rock from space traveling through the atmosphere at high speed. Meteors burn and form streaks of light as they fall to Earth.

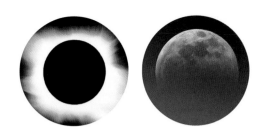

microbes living things too small to see without a microscope.

mold a filmy or fuzzy fungus (an organism that resembles a plant, but has no leaves, flowers, or roots) that grows on damp or decaying surfaces.

molecules the smallest possible particles of a substance.

molten melted by heat. Lava is molten rock.

partial eclipse (of the Sun) occurs when the Moon passes between the Sun and Earth so that part of the Sun's light is blocked out.

solar eclipse occurs when the Moon comes between the Sun and Earth so that all or part of the Sun's light is blocked out.

solid a state of matter with a definite shape and volume.

speed of impact the speed that an object is traveling when it hits a surface.

sphere a shape like a basketball or a globe. All points of the shape are the same distance from the center of the shape.

spores plant cells that develop into new plants. Spores are produced by plants that do not flower, such as fungi, mosses, and ferns.

static electricity electricity that builds up in an object and stays there. Static electricity can be produced when one object rubs against another.

sublimation the process of causing a solid or gas to change state without becoming liquid.

suction the act of drawing air out of a space to create a vacuum. This causes the surrounding air or liquid to be sucked into the empty space. Vacuum cleaners and drinking straws work by suction.

surface tension a pulling force caused by the strong attraction between water molecules.

temperature a measure of heat energy.

tornado a violent, spinning funnel of air that appears as a dark cloud shaped like a funnel. A tornado travels fast and usually destroys everything in its narrow path.

vacuum a sealed space from which all air or gas has been emptied.

vent (volcanic) the shaft of a volcano through which smoke and lava escape.

vortex a powerful, swirling current of air or water.

waterspout a tornado that forms over water.

water vapor the gas produced when water evaporates.

whirlpools swirling currents of water that move quickly in a circle and pull floating objects toward their center.

xylems water-conducting tissues of a plant.

Pictures are shown in **bold**.

Photographs © 2008: age fotostock/Tom Hoenig: 4 right, 19; AGStockUSA/Mike Boyatt: 12 bottom; Corbis Images: 8 (Eric Nguyen), 4 center left, 10 right, 29 (Paul Steeger/zefa); Getty Images: 24, 26 left (G. Brad Lewis), 5 right, 25 bottom (Jim Sugar), 5 center, 11 (Tartan Dragon Ltd.); Photo Researchers, NY: 14 (Van Bucher), 9 right (J.G. Golden), 21 (NASA), 18 top, 31 right (David Nunuk), 22 bottom (Pekka Parviainen), 5 center left, 16, 31 left (John Sanford), 13 top (Charles D. Winters), 3 bottom right, 5 left, 27 (Kent Wood); Richard Hutchings Photography: cover, back cover, 3 top right, 3 top left, 4 left, 4 center right, 5 center right, 6, 7, 9 left, 10 left, 12 top, 13 bottom, 15, 18 bottom, 20, 22 top, 23 bottom, 25 top, 26 right, 28; ShutterStock, Inc./Lena Grottling: 3 center right, 23 top.